IoT With M5Stack and UIFlow - Volume 1

UIFlow Version 1.9.X

Written By Adam Bryant.

Introduction.

When I started writing this Internet of Things guide (hereafter abbreviated to IoT,) I was only concerned with understanding the functions available from within UIFlow however, after fighting with Microsoft Azure and a general lack of understanding of how the IoT functions worked, Facebook member Sukesh Ashok Kumar came up with the following suggestion:

Sukesh Ashok Kumar
Pick a practical scenario based project so twins etc makes sense.

If home automation, map every smart device/equipment to twins, then managing from remote becomes a breeze.

Like   Reply   13 h

Taking this comment to heart, I decided that I would use my greenhouse electronic project as the scenario for this IoT guide and so you will see repetition of the project setup for giving examples on the various functions.

Thank you Sukesh for giving me a sense of direction for this guide.

What Is IoT?

Internet of Things (IoT) is a collection of hardware and software that is used to allow devices to connect to each other over the Internet in order to send data and commands to each other.

What devices produced by M5Stack can be used for IoT?

Surprisingly most of the M5Stack controllers from the Core 2 series to the ATOM and Stamp Series can be used for IoT as long as they have access to the internet via wifi. Not only can the controllers be used for IoT but some units now use the ESP32 microcontroller used in the main M5Stack Controllers.

What software is needed for IoT?

IoT software is split into two main categories, Firmware and Remote Services.

Firmware (in the case of this book) is created in UIFlow and uploaded to the controllers and Remote Services is software installed to servers that can be in the same wifi network on servers hosted in the cloud (internet for us oldies).

What hardware will I be using for this guide?

Throughout the guide you will see me using the same hardware for the various projects. This hardware is mostly purchased from M5Stack and will have links to the products on the Official M5Stack store. Where products are not made by M5Stack I will provide a link to the Amazon UK shop as an example location to buy them.

M5Stack Controllers.

Core2/ Core2 AWS

Here I will mostly be using the Core2 AWS as my Core2 is in use on other projects. I am recommending the Core2 series as they have more ram than the Core, Stick, Atom and, stamp series but I have just managed to get the Atom to run on AWS IoT services.

To Purchase a Core2:
https://shop.m5stack.com/collections/m5-controllers/products/m5stack-core2-esp32-iot-development-kit?ref=pfpqkvphmgr

To purchase a Core 2 AWS:
https://shop.m5stack.com/collections/m5-controllers/products/
m5stack-core2-esp32-iot-development-kit-for-aws-iot-edukit?
ref=pfpqkvphmgr

M5Stack Sensors.

ENV Sensor

While you can use any of the ENV sensor versions, I am using the ENV3 Unit and it was brought just for this series of projects. The ENV sensor is connected to port A of the Core2 AWS.

In UIFlow there are three functions available that return the Temperature, Pressure and humidity.

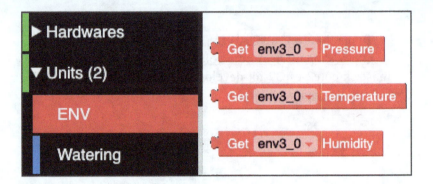

In order to use these blocks we need to create a simple script that contains three labels to show the values as shown below.

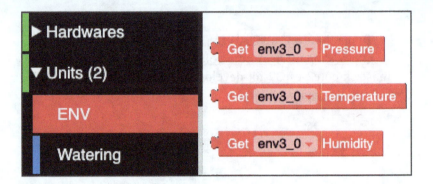

This is only a simple example and later in the book I will show you how to extend this example for the various IoT services.

To purchase the ENV Sensor from M5Stack, please visit:
https://shop.m5stack.com/collections/m5-sensor/products/env-iii-unit-with-temperature-humidity-air-pressure-sensor-sht30-qmp6988?ref=pfpqkvphmgr&variant=40187936309420

Watering Unit

The Watering Sensor consist of a small water pump and capacitive moisture sensor built into one unit that is connected to the Cores using Port B of the Core2's base. The pump comes with two short hoses but the inlet and outlet is compatible with 4.6mm (3/16") irrigation hoses and accessories from companies like Gardena, Hozelock and others that uses the 4.6mm (3/16") irrigation hose size.

In UIFlow the Watering Unit has 1 value block and two function blocks:

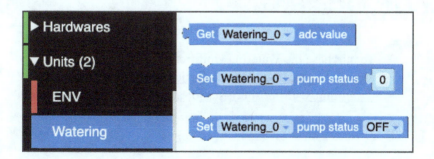

We can use code similar to the ENV3 example to read the moisture sensor on the unit:

However, to control the pump we need a few more blocks.

To purchase the Watering Unit from M5Stack, please visit:
https://shop.m5stack.com/collections/m5-sensor/products/
watering-unit-with-mositure-sensor-and-pump?ref=pfpqkvphmgr

While the Soil Moisture sensor could be used in the projects it is not recommended. These sensors are resistive and have exposed copper in order to sense moisture levels. This exposed copper means that they have a short life as the copper gets corroded.

If you wish to use this in UIFLow, the unit only has two blocks that return values:

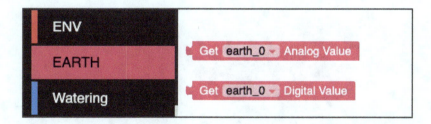

And we can use code similar to the ENV sensor example code:

To purchase the Soil Moisture Sensor from M5Stack, please visit:

https://shop.m5stack.com/collections/m5-sensor/products/earth-sensor-unit?ref=pfpqkvphmgr&variant=16804783882330

The Scenario.

The scenario that I will be using for all the IoT examples is that the Core2 AWS will act as the Greenhouses IoT Hub, the sensors and pumps will connect to the Core2 AWS that will send the data to and from the sensors to the IoT services and react on preset events triggering the pumps.

Below is a simple diagram of how the hardware is connected together.

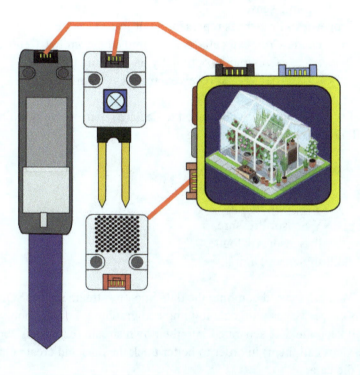

Data Collection.

In order to understand the data collected by the Core2 that is sent to the IoT services, the information needs to be separated in to data categories.

These categories are as follows:

Telemetry - Telemetry is a stream of values sent from the device, typically from a sensor.
Properties - Properties represent point-in-time values.
Commands - You can call device commands from IoT Central. Commands optionally pass parameters to the device and receive a response from the device.

For this project to work I need to declare telemetry values that will need to be collected will be

- Wartering Unit Moisture,
- ENV Sensor Temperature,
- ENV Sensor Humidity,
- ENV Sensor Pressure,
- Earth Sensor Analogue,
- Earth Sensor Digital.

While we could combine the data into one stream using JSON, this causes issues with data logging and graphing. For this book I will keep the data separated into their own stream (or feed as some services call them) in order to better track the data and create charts of the data.

In addition to the telemetry values I will also need to define commands for:

- Watering Unit Pump,
- Core2 LED Colours.

In each of the services I will show you how to collect the telemetry data and control the pumps and LEDS.

Security Features

While most IoT services provide encryption and secure connections using SSL, there appears to be a few issues with security implementation in UIFlow as of writing and so I will mostly be using the basic access methods throughout this volume.

M5Stack EZData (Part 1)

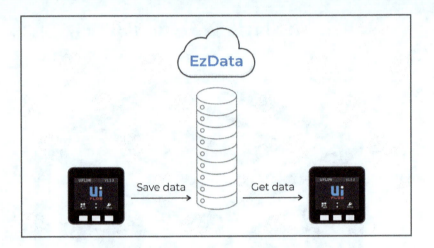

Introduction to M5Stack EZData.

EZData is an IoT solution provided by M5Stack using their own servers that allows us to send data from one device to another device via the cloud and an internet connection.

Save Value to Topic With Token.

The Save Value to Topic with Token block is used to send data from an M5Stack devices to the EZData service instance defined with the random generated token. The token is generated in UIFlow and automatically placed in the block when the block is added to a program.

The following example retrieves the temperature from the ENV3 sensor Unit and writes it to the topic Temperature on the EZData server.

When run with a valid token the results on the EZData server is as follows:

Clicking on the bin icon will delete the topic, the arrow icon creates links to the data that has been sent to the server and the Bar chart icon shows a chart of readings:

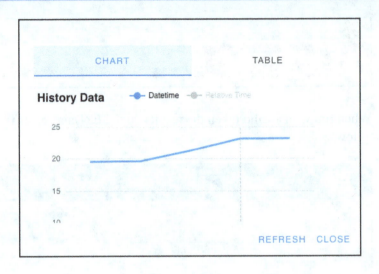

While clicking on "Table" shows the transmitted data also know as telemetry:

Datetime	Value
2022-02-24 18:09:50	23.14946
2022-02-24 18:09:47	23.12009
2022-02-24 17:57:17	21.25887

Get Value from Topic with Token

The Get Value from Topic with Token block is used for retrieving data from the EZData service. Unlike the Save Value block which is a function, the Get value requires additional blocks to work like a label block. The following example uses another Label to retrieve data from the EZdata topic temperature.

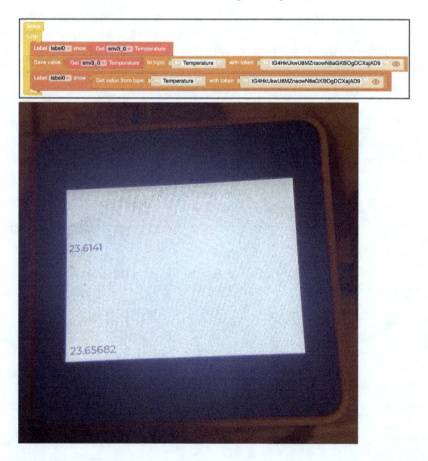

Remove Topic

In order to remove a topic from EZData you can click on the Bin icon in EZData page or you can use the following block in UIFLow:

The Remove Topic block takes the name of the the topic you want to remove and the token that points to the individual server instance that is assigned to you.

Save Value to List

So far I have just shown how to write, retrieve and delete single entries. Next I will show you how to work with lists in EZData. To start using lists we need to create one using the following block:

If we add the Save Value To List block to the existing code:

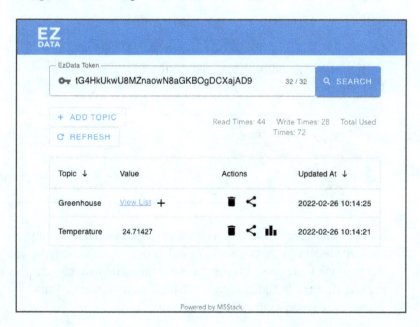

We get the following in EZData:

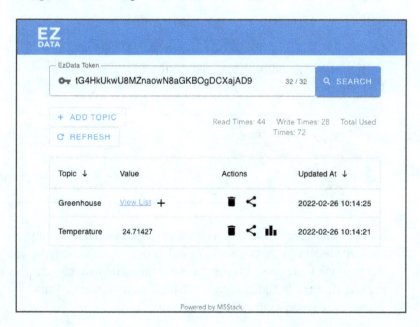

Clicking on "View List" brings up the following:

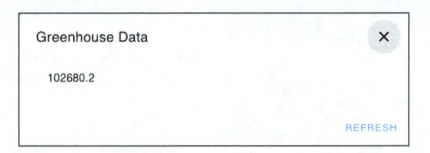

Greenhouse Data

102680.2

REFRESH

Unfortunately, if we try to add the other readings from the ENV3 to the list, the Core2 will crash without an error and only the first entry sent to the list will appear.

A second issue with the list is that for some reason when the "List block" is used, the "Get Value from topic block" fails to retrieve any data.

Get Value From List

To retrieve an entry from a list we use the "Get Value From List" block:

The "Get value from list" is used to define which list you want to retrieve data from, "Offset" is used to define which entry in the list you want retrieved, "Count" is how many items you want from the list after the initial entry and "With Token" is the EZData instance assigned to the UIFlow session.

In the following list example I added some random entries to the list to make it easier to see:

GreenHouse Temperature Data   ✕

    Temperature:21.72617

    ERROR:ENOMOM

    Temp:ERROR

    Temperature:22.04929

    Temperature:21.58198

    23.86778

                                     REFRESH

When I run the following modified example:

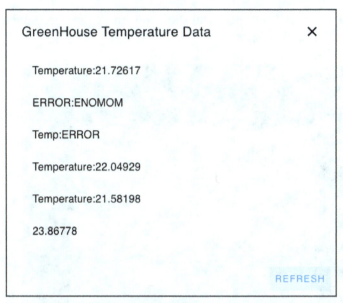

The Core2 AWS display will show the third entry because the offset starts at 0 and not 1.

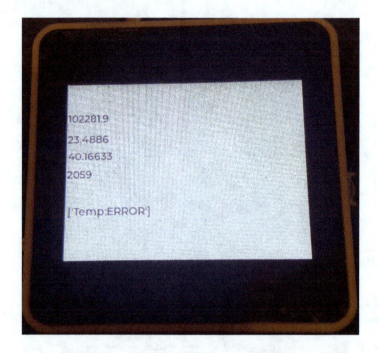

Get Current ISODateTime

The last block to be found in the first section of EZData block is the "Get Current ISODateTime" block.

Get current ISODateTime

The "Get Current ISODateTime" retrieves the timestamp for the EZData instance clock supplied by the servers own clock.

In the following example I have replaced the cable that was showing the pressure with the "Get Current ISODateTime":

Which when run shows the current server time.

Microsoft Azure

Introduction.

While Microsoft Azure offer a free service, you may find yourself quickly growing out of this free level and getting charged as Azure is aimed for the more business end of the IoT market.

Azure is an exercise in utter frustration if you are only getting started and the M5Stack FB group has been on the receiving end of my many frustrations.

In order to get started with Azure, you need to register. If you haven't already, follow all the on-screen prompts to register and then you will end up at the dashboard

In order to get started we first need to create a resource. Click on the "Create a Resource" and the next screen will appear.

Type Resource into the search box and hit enter.

Click on Resource,

Click on the "Create" Button,

Give the resource a name and select the region of the world you are in (in my case I'm in the west of the UK and so chose UK West). Next click on "Next: Tags" .

Click on the empty box's and select the items that appear as default and then click on the Review create button.

Double check the setting are correct and then click on "Create".

Now that we have created a resource group we can now create an IoT Hub. Click on the IoT Hub Icon to be take to the IoT Hub page.

This page is normally empty as there won't have been a hub created yet.

Click on the "Create" button and the hub creation window will open.

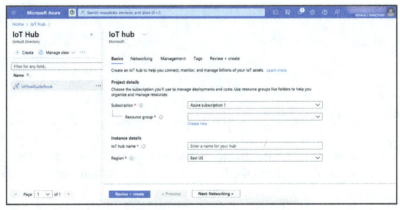

Leave "Azure subscription 1" box as it is, click on the dropdown arrow to select a resource group, then click on "Next: Networking".

Leave this as Public and click "Next:Management".

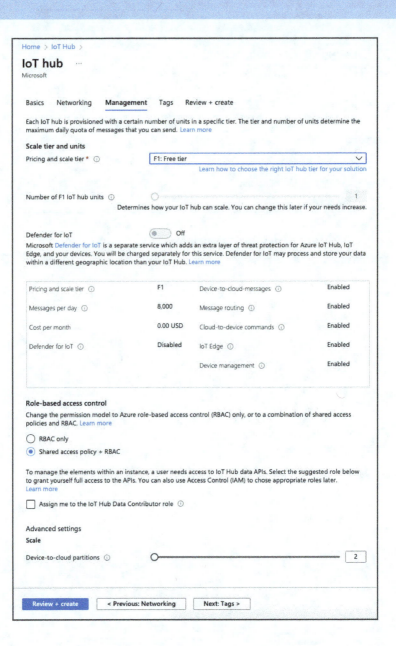

Home > IoT Hub >

IoT hub ⋯
Microsoft

Basics   Networking   **Management**   Tags   Review + create

Each IoT hub is provisioned with a certain number of units in a specific tier. The tier and number of units determine the maximum daily quota of messages that you can send. Learn more

Scale tier and units

Pricing and scale tier * ⓘ   F1: Free tier   ⌄

Learn how to choose the right IoT hub tier for your solution

Number of F1 IoT hub units ⓘ   ○   1

Determines how your IoT hub can scale. You can change this later if your needs increase.

Defender for IoT   ◯ Off

Microsoft Defender for IoT is a separate service which adds an extra layer of threat protection for Azure IoT Hub, IoT Edge, and your devices. You will be charged separately for this service. Defender for IoT may process and store your data within a different geographic location than your IoT Hub. Learn more

Pricing and scale tier ⓘ	F1	Device-to-cloud-messages ⓘ	Enabled
Messages per day ⓘ	8,000	Message routing ⓘ	Enabled
Cost per month	0.00 USD	Cloud-to-device commands ⓘ	Enabled
Defender for IoT ⓘ	Disabled	IoT Edge ⓘ	Enabled
		Device management ⓘ	Enabled

Role-based access control

Change the permission model to Azure role-based access control (RBAC) only, or to a combination of shared access policies and RBAC. Learn more

○ RBAC only

◉ Shared access policy + RBAC

To manage the elements within an instance, a user needs access to IoT Hub data APIs. Select the suggested role below to grant yourself full access to the APIs. You can also use Access Control (IAM) to chose appropriate roles later. Learn more

☐ Assign me to the IoT Hub Data Contributor role ⓘ

Advanced settings
Scale

Device-to-cloud partitions ⓘ   O━━━━━━━━━━━━━━━━   2

[Review + create]   [< Previous: Networking]   [Next: Tags >]

Change the Pricing and Scale tier to "F1: Free tier", then scroll down and click on the box next to "Assign me to the IoT Hub Data Contributor role", then click on "Next: Tags".

Click on the box's again to assign the tags and then click the "Next: Review + Create" button.

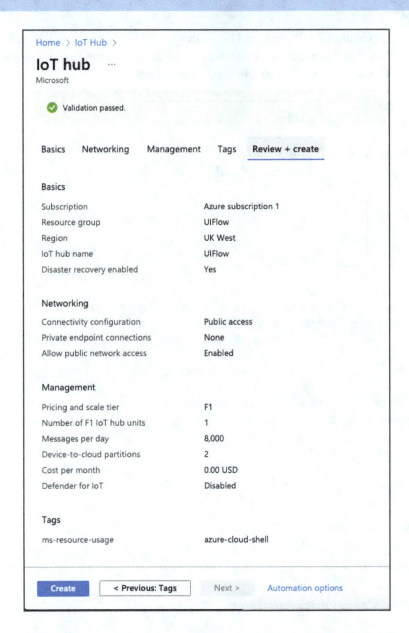

Home > IoT Hub >

IoT hub ...

Microsoft

✓ Validation passed.

| Basics | Networking | Management | Tags | **Review + create** |

Basics

Subscription	Azure subscription 1
Resource group	UIFlow
Region	UK West
IoT hub name	UIFlow
Disaster recovery enabled	Yes

Networking

Connectivity configuration	Public access
Private endpoint connections	None
Allow public network access	Enabled

Management

Pricing and scale tier	F1
Number of F1 IoT hub units	1
Messages per day	8,000
Device-to-cloud partitions	2
Cost per month	0.00 USD
Defender for IoT	Disabled

Tags

ms-resource-usage	azure-cloud-shell

| Create | < Previous: Tags | Next > | Automation options |

Review the setting and then click on "Create" to create the hub.

Deployment may take a while but when it is finished, you will have a button appear at the bottom that will take to back to the IoT Hub page.

The page now shows the IoT Hub created and a set of charts showing various metrics. At the moment, nothing will appear in the charts because we haven't connected any devices.

Now that the resources and hub have been created, it is time to add a device. Click on the IoT Hub and then click on the hub created earlier to open it.

Under device management, click on "Devices" to open the device page. To create a device click on "+ Add Device".

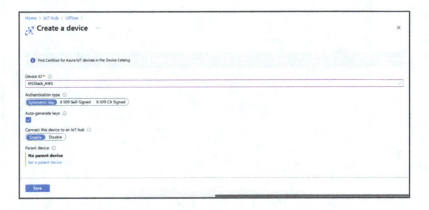

Type in a name which Azure will use to identify the device. In this guide I am using an M5Stack Core2 AWS and so I just type "M5Stack_AWS".

Make sure all other settings are as shown and press save to create the device and return to the devices page.

If the device ID doesn't appear, wait a few seconds and then click refresh, this reloads the page listing the device as the page doesn't always get refreshed during creation.

Next click on the Device ID to load the devices options.

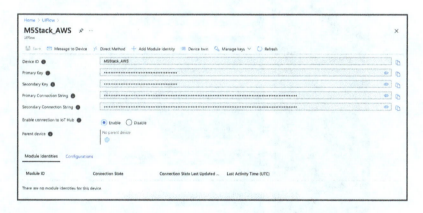

This will bring up this page showing the connection keys that will be needed for connecting hardware.

And that is everything needed to set up the Azure IOT server. Next it is time for the M5Stack side of programming.

Azure IoT UIFlow Blocks.

The UIFlow blocks used to access Azure IOT services are found in UIFlow under the IoT Cloud Menu:

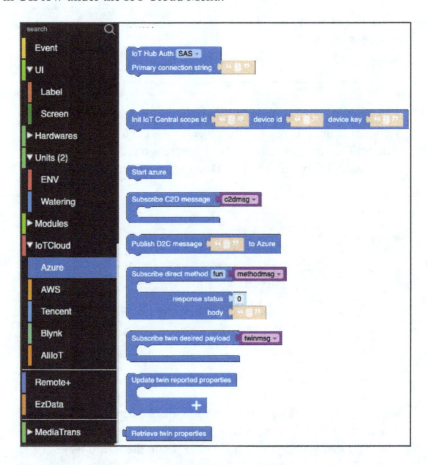

In order to test the connection to Azure IoT Hub I used the following example:

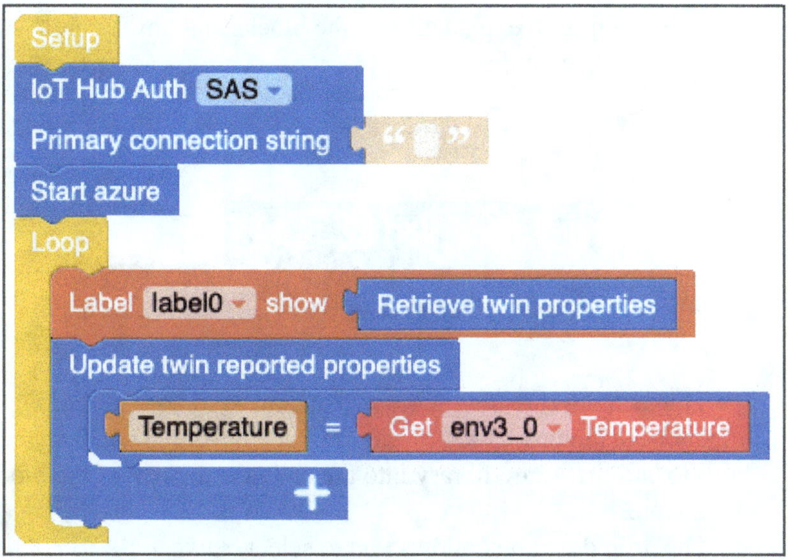

This simple Example sent two values ENV and the temperature reading to Azure. In order to view the reading we need to look at the JSON data under device twin in the Azure IoT Hub webpage:

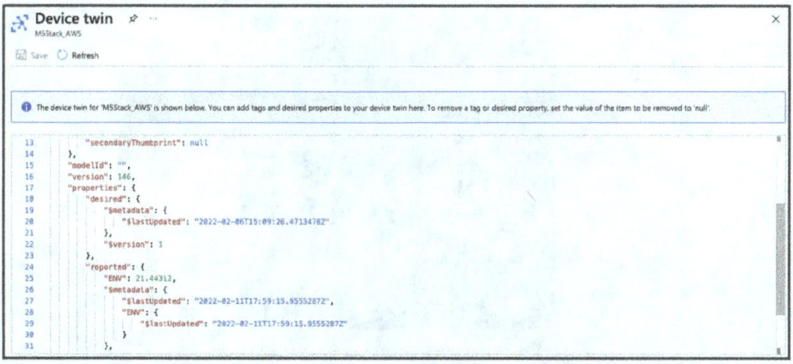

The screen shot shows how the data is sent but, in order for other services to interact with the data the information needs to be edited.

Following is an explanation of the blocks and how to build an example code with them.

IoT Hub SAS Authentication

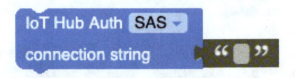

This Is the Azure config block that is used to hold the settings Azure needs in order to allow an M5Stack device to connect and also to call the Azure library into the code for the rest of the blocks to operate.

The drop down box allows you to select between SAS or X.509 as the authentication method and the text box is used to hold the connection string that need to be generated before connecting a hardware device to the Azure IoT Cloud.

IoT Hub X.509 Authentication

The Connection String box is where you type in the Primary connection string which UIFlow uses to generate the SAS keys during runtime.

The Micropython code for the SAS block consist of only one line:

azure = IoT_Hub(connection_string=' ')

While the X509 block consists of the following code:

azure = IoT_Hub(device_id=, host_name=, ssl=True, cert_file_path=", private_key_path=' ')

I need to point out that when the config block is added to the program, a new import function consisting of the following line:

from IoTcloud.Azure import IoT_Hub

is added to the list of imported functions.already visible in Micropython.

from m5stack import *
from m5stack_ui import *
from uiflow import *
from IoTcloud.Azure import IoT_Hub

Next we have the IoT Hub Central connection block.

IoT Central Connection Block.

Unlike the previous SAS block that needs only the primary Key, the IoT Hub Central block needs three values that are obtained when we try to connect to hardware from within the IoT Hub Central App.

Next we have the Azure Start block.

Azure Start

This block must be placed outside and before any program loops as it can only be run once. Placing it inside a loop will result in the Azure program trying to open multiple new connections to the Azure IoT Cloud and will result in the device being blocked as it could be perceived to be an attack attempt.

The Micropython code for this block is as follows:

azure.start()

Subscribe C2D Message

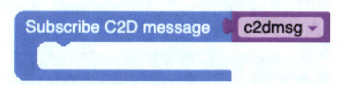

C2D is an abbreviation of Cloud to Device and is used to send messages from Azure web services to devices.

Subscribe C2D Message connects to a message server and is used to receive message.

The Miscropython code for this block is

```
def azure_C2D_cb(msg_data):
  global c2dmsg
  c2dmsg = msg_data
  pass
```

Publish D2C Message

Publish D2C is used to send data to the Azure cloud message system.

The Miscropython code for this block is

```
azure.publish_D2C_message(str())
```

Subscribe Direct Method

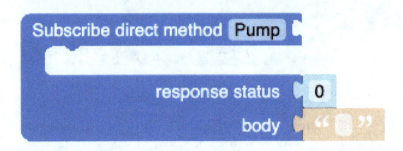

def azure_direct_Pump(payload, rid):
 global pumpmsg
 _ = payload

azure.response_direct_method(0, rid, body=")

Subscribe Twin Desired Payload.

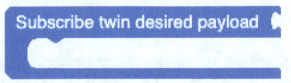

Subscribes to the Azure Device Twin system with the specified payload.

def azure_desired_cb(payload):
 global pumpmsg
 pumpmsg = payload

Update Twin Reported Properties.

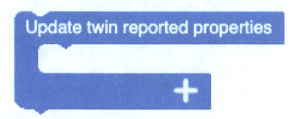

Used to update properties in the Azure Device Twin

If you click on the "+" sign a block will appear to allow you send a Key and value pair.

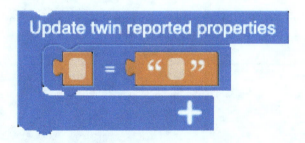

Retrieve Twin Properties.

Retrieve Twin Properties returns the values received by Azure's Device Twin system

Creating an IoT Central Applications.

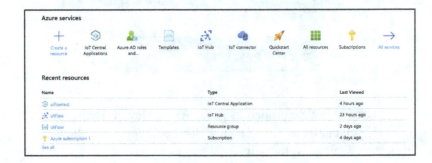

From The IoT hub locate IoT Central Applications and click on it to open the IoT Central page.

Click on "+ Create" to start creating a new application.

Give the resource a name but it must be all lowercase as the name will be used for the web address to the application.

Chose a Subscription. In my case I only had one choice.

Choose a Resource group. The Resource group I chose I created earlier in the guide.

Select a Pricing plan, Standard 2 allows up to two free devices to connect to the application.

Set Location to the location in the world you are based in.

After filling in the required boxes click on "Create"

Wait for deployment to finish and when the "Goto Resource" button appears, click on it.

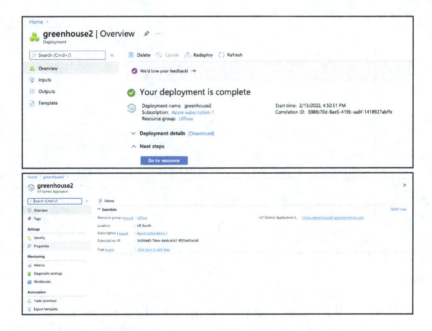

To view the application and to begin customising the application, click on the link to the right of the page.

The application screen will open to show the following

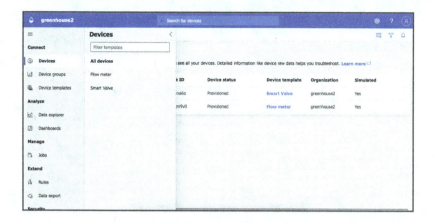

Here we can see that the page has been populated with examples that show us how the application has been built. Along with virtual devices that are used to simulate data.

If we click on a device we can see several pages of information and device data layouts.

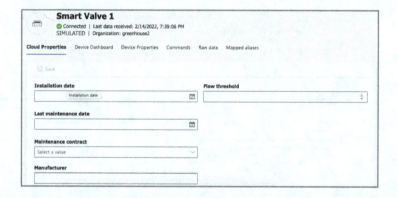

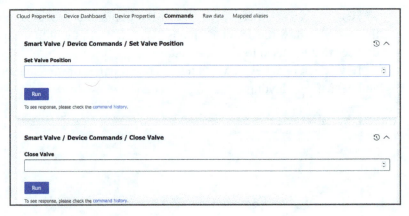

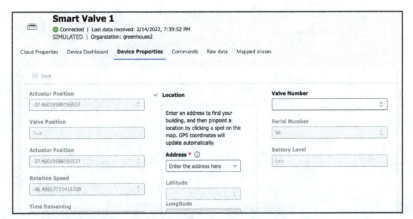

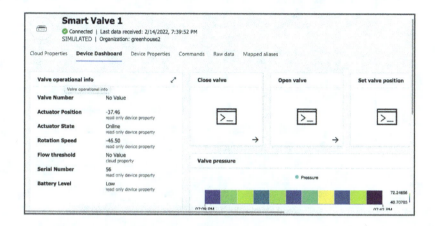

And if we go to Device Templates:

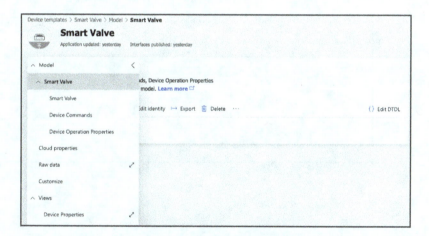

We can see various screens that show how the data is to be sorted and reacted on by the application.

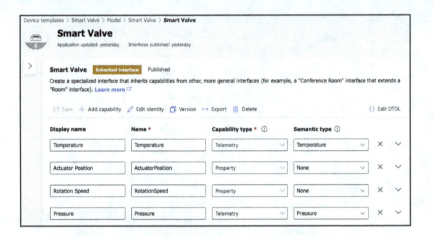

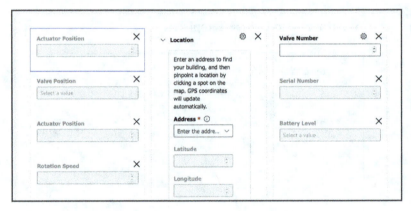

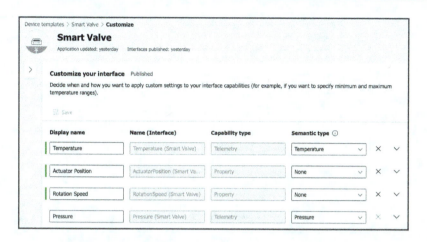

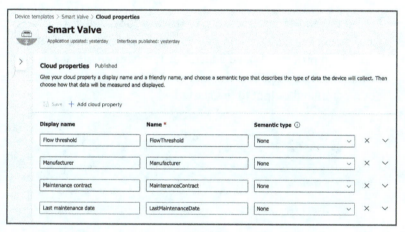

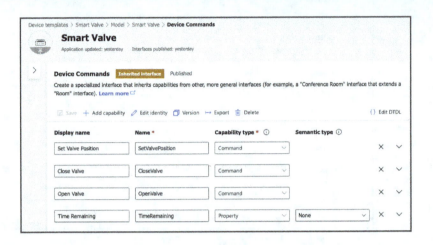

At the end of this book I have made a form which you can copy and print to make notes on the various functions you will need in your own projects. I have added the Temperature device as an example of an input and the moisture sensor/pump as an example of a command/output to get started.

Azure IoT Planner

Display Name	Name	Capability	Semantic Type	Schema
Shown as Data type Heading.	Data Type Name.	Property, Telemetry, Command	Type of reading (Temp, Pressure,Speed, etc)	Double, Float, Integra or Long
Temperature	Temperature	Telemetry	Temperature	Double
Water Pump	Pump	Command	N/A	N/A

In the following picture I have the initial hardware set up in a basic configuration. Unfortunately the Core2 AWS only has one Port A and One Port B and so I can only connect the ENV to port A and the moisture Sensor/Pump to port B.

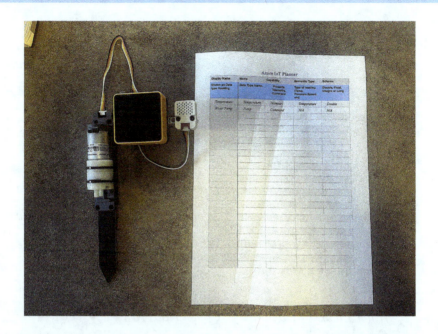

Next to the hardware is the planner form. The two example entries are for the hardware but more entries are needed. In the following table I list the additional entries that need to be added:

Azure IoT Planner-1

Display Name	Name	Capability	Semantic Type	Schema
Shown as Data type Heading.	Data Type Name.	Property, Telemetry, Command	Type of reading (Temp, Pressure, Speed, etc)	Double, Float, Integra or Long
Humidity	Humidity	Telemetry	Percent	Double
Pressure	Pressure	Telemetry	Pascal	Double
Temperature	Temperature	Telemetry	Temperature	Double
Moisture Sensor	Moisture	Telemetry	Percent	Double
Water Pump On	PumpOn	Command	N/A	N/A
Water Pump Off	PumpOff	Command	N/A	N/A

Now that I have made a list of the functions I need in the Azure application, we need to set the Azure IoT Application to receive and handle the date to be received from the Core2 AWS.

Reopen the Azure Application and go to the Templates Section and delete the existing templates. As we made a list of the functions we need (shown above) based on the information in those templates, we don't need them any more.

Click on the "New" button at the top of the screen to start creating the new template:

This opens the Template creation panel that allows us to create a new IoT device template, create an IoT Edge device template, or import an existing device template. As no template exist for the Core2 AWS or any other M5Stack device, we need to click on the IoT device button.

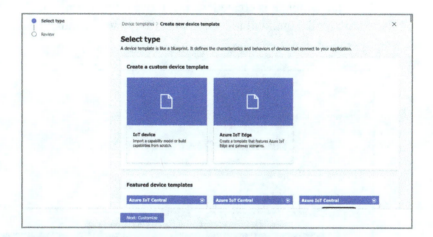

Click on "IoT Device" and then click on the "Customise" button that appears at the bottom of the screen to move on.

Give the template a name and then click the "Next: Review" button to move on:

As this shows what we have filled in so far, click on the "Create" button to make the template.

Now the template is created we can move on to adding the hardware model that will tell the application how to handle the data being sent to it.

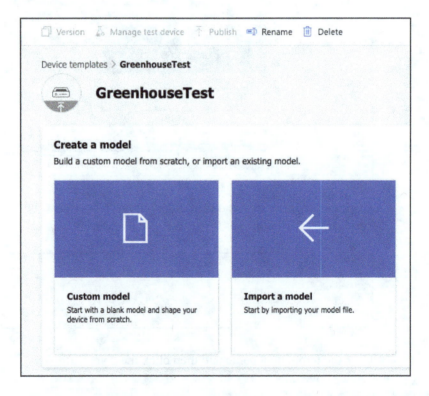

Click on "Custom Model" and this take us to the page allowing us to set up how the data will be handled.

Click on "+ Add Capability" button to start adding the functions.

Here I show how the inputs are handled. The way the "Name" is typed here is important as this tells the application what part of the data contains what.

Setting these to properties will allow them to be shown in the data of the Application:

Interface / Hu...	Interface / Moi...	Interface / Pre...	Interface / Te...
48.59083	2063	100541.4	22.71152
48.37873	2064	100541.9	22.65545
48.50385	2062	100543	22.58335
48.59388	2062	100540.1	22.68215
48.61219	2064	100539.5	22.6688
48.52674	2063	100539.6	22.68215
48.59388	2043	100539.7	22.55665
48.61829	2063	100537.6	22.61272
48.65034	2060	100535.1	22.65545
48.44434	2061	100534.5	22.72488

This must be exactly as typed in the "Twin Properties" box in UIFlow or the data will not be recognised.

Clicking on the arrow next to each function we create allows us to customise the function by setting the units that the function data is being sent in and the application needs to show it as.

Skip down to views, click on create view, give the view a name and drag four bar graphs onto the area on the right which will be used to display data sent from the Core2 AWS to the application.

Click on the pencil icon to open the configuration for each bar graph, give each a different name and click on the "+ Add Capability" button to select the telemetry stream you wish it to show.

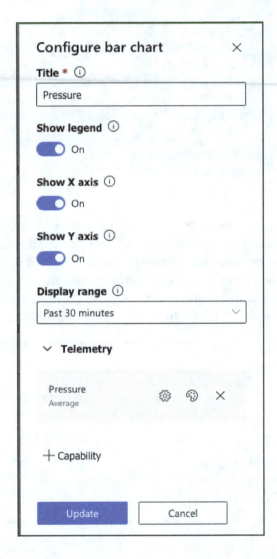

Click on "Update" to apply the setting to the bar graphs and once all four are set, click on the "Save button to save and close the view window returning us to the main template window. Ignore the commands functions I have added in my screen shots and click on "Publish" at the top of the screen to make the template live.

Next go to "Devices" and click on the "+New" button to create a new device:

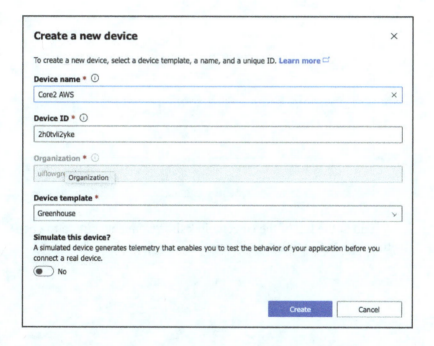

Give the device a unique name, set the template to the template we just created and then click on the "Create" Button.

Click on the device to open it:

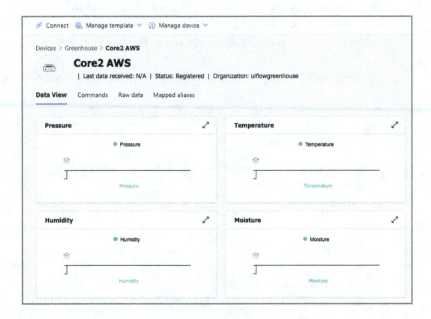

and at the top of the screen click the "Connect" button to open the page containing the connection keys:

Device connection groups   ✕

ID scope ⓘ

0ne004E47B3

Device ID ⓘ

2h0tvli2yke

Choose the connection type for this device. You can change this later if you need to.

Authentication type

Shared access signature (SAS)   ⌄

Key   QR code

Shared Access Signatures (SAS) use security tokens and keys to connect to IoT Central. Use the SAS keys from the default enrollment group shown below to register your device.
Learn more ⌐

Primary key ⓘ

vi+g5bBJ5PFDzSpk58rOfJXKJ6ZEw/G3WygN0uZZ9pw=

Secondary key ⓘ

j9e/M0uxOChLs5BN3xWgfZs52QfU0gAQO/VymQj7hEs=

Close

Make a note of these keys and strings as they will need to be entered into the IoT Central connection block of the UIFlow code. Click on close and now we can more on to UIFLow and start creating the code.

First we start by merging the two example programs given in the hardware section into one program:

```
Setup
  Set Watering_0 ▾ pump status  0
Loop
  Label label0 ▾ show  Get env3_0 ▾ Pressure
  Label label1 ▾ show  Get env3_0 ▾ Temperature
  Label label2 ▾ show  Get env3_0 ▾ Humidity
  Label label3 ▾ show  Get Watering_0 ▾ adc value
  if    Get Watering_0 ▾ adc value  < ▾  100
  do    Set Watering_0 ▾ pump status  1
  else  Set Watering_0 ▾ pump status  0
  Wait  500  ms
```

Next we need to connect the Core2 AWS to The Azure example application using the Azure IoT Central Connection block and then add the updated Twin Properties block that sends the captured data to the Azure Application.

```
Setup
  IoT Hub Auth  SAS
  Primary connection string  " "
  Set  Watering_0  pump status  0
  Start azure
  Loop
    Label  label0  show  Get  env3_0  Pressure
    Label  label1  show  Get  env3_0  Temperature
    Label  label2  show  Get  env3_0  Humidity
    Label  label3  show  Get  Watering_0  adc value
    Update twin reported properties
        Temperature  =  Get  env3_0  Temperature
        +
    Wait  500  ms
    if    Get  Watering_0  adc value  <  100
    do    Set  Watering_0  pump status  1
    else  Set  Watering_0  pump status  0
```

Copy the code as shown above, replace the Scope ID, Device ID and Device key with your own keys and save the program to the Core2 AWS so that it starts running and sending data.

Alas, as the Azure IoT Central is only free for 30 days, I am unable to get the pump working and continue using the Azure services without paying.

Maybe one day when finances are more willing I may be able to revisit Azure services but until then I apologise for not being able to finished the Azure side of the guide.

Amazon Web Services (AWS)

Introduction.

To use the Amazon Web Services Internet of Things (AWS IOT onwards) you first need to register with the AWS site. If you have an Amazon account then you can now sign in with these credentials.

Once you log in and win the fight with captcha, you will be taken to this page:

This page will gave you some getting started guides and a list of costs you may build up once you start using the services.

At the top of the screen next to the name you registered as you will find a location, this must be set your geographically local region or you may get some unexpected finical charges. Another note about the region servers is that not all AWS services are available to all regions.

Next click on the search bar and type in "IOT"

This will bring up a list of AWS services that match the search string:

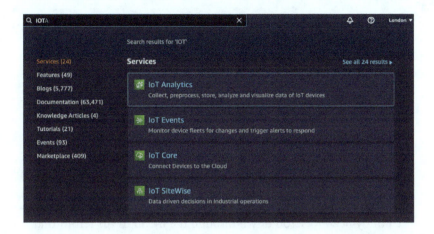

We will be using IOT Core in this guide and so click on IOT Core to be taken to the AWS IOT service.

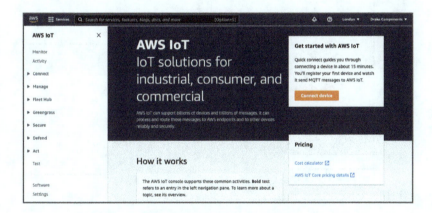

It is worth looking through the guides and documents in order to understand the IOT service and how to use it before moving on.

In order for a device (or thing as AWS calls them,) to connect to the AWS services we have to create the thing, attach security certificates, polices and rules and then program them into the device. While the AWS Console used to set up the device has changed, the instruction created by M5Stack found here: https://

<u>docs.m5stack.com/en/uiflow/iotcloud/aws</u> along with the UIFLOW example is still valid.

There is a little variation between the M5Stack guide and my guide but, that is because I hope to clear up some issues that new users may have including describing the various blocks available in UIFLOW.

Before we can create a thing that is the AWS IOT representation of the M5Stack, we need to create a policy which allows the M5Stack to communicate with the AWS IOT service. To create a policy need to scroll down through the menu of the left to find secure, click on it to open the menu and click on policy.

▼ **Secure**

   Overview

   Certificates

   Policies

   CAs

   Role Aliases

   Authorizers

This opens the policy page:

Here you can see that I already have a policy created but I will still show you how to create the policy.

Click on the "Create Policy" button:

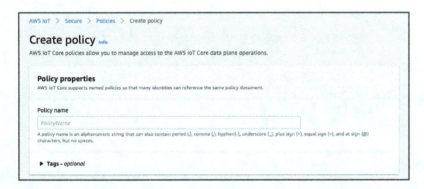

Give the policy a name and in the next box, click on JSON to open the policy rules panel.

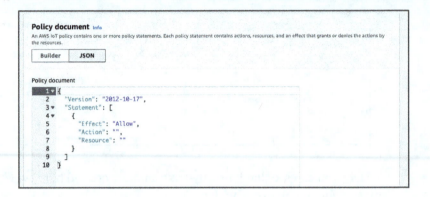

In the code box change:

```
{
  "Version": "2012-10-17",
  "Statement": [
    {
      "Effect": "Allow",
      "Action": "",
      "Resource": ""
    }
  ]
}
```

To

```
{
  "Version": "2012-10-17",
  "Statement": [
    {
      "Effect": "Allow",
      "Action": "iot:*",
      "Resource": "*"
    }
  ]
}
```

Click on "create" to create the policy and return to the policy page that will now show out newly created policy.

Now the policy is created we can now create a thing. Scroll up to "Manage" and click on "Things" to open the Things page:

Click on the "Create Thing" button to open the create thing page:

Click on "Create Single Thing" and then click on the "Next" Button.

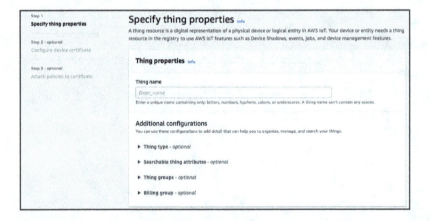

Give the thing a name, leave all setting as they are and then scroll down and click the "Next" button to move on.

As this is the first time you are setting up a thing make sure that "Auto-generate a new certificate (recommended)" is selected before clicking on "Next"

This page allows us to select the policy that was created earlier. (Here I am using the existing policy).

Clicking on "Create Thing" will create the thing and bring up the device certificates.

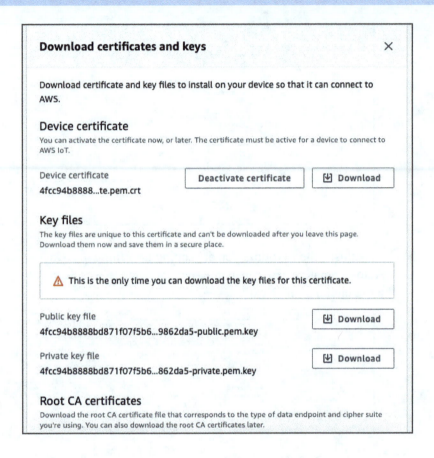

Important note: These keys and codes do not work on my account As they are now deactivated and now deleted!

Download the Certificates and keys and then click on "Done" to close the panel and return to the Thing page sowing our newly created thing.

And that is everything needed to set up the AWS IOT server. Next it is time for the M5Stack side of programming.

The UIFlow blocks used to access AWS IOT services are found in UIFlow. Following is an explanation of the blocks and how to build an example code with them.

This Is the AWS config block that is used to hold the settings AWS needs in order to allow an M5Stack device to connect and also to call the AWS library into the code for the rest of the blocks to operate.

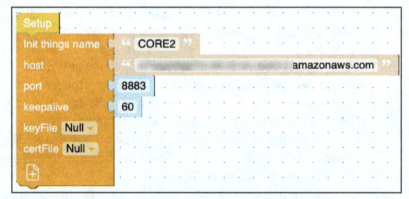

Init Things Name is used to connect a text block that will hold a name you give to you device. This name must be matched on the AWS IoT page:

The Host block is used to hold the AWS Endpoint that your thing will used to connect to AWS:

Port number has to be set to 8883 according to this AWS page https://docs.aws.amazon.com/iot/latest/developerguide/protocols.html

The **Keepalive block** is used to set a time in seconds that a connection will be kept open between a device and the AWS services. If not set, the the connection between the device and AWS will be closed if there is no messages being set from the device.

The Key file drop down menu is used to select any Private Key files stored on the M5Stack device. This must be set to the Private key file that must be named as **Private.Pem.key.**

The Certfile drop down menu is used to select the device certificate that must be named **Certificate.pem.cert**.

The keys and certificates are generated by AWS when you create you policies needed for a device to connect to AWS services.

The icon on the bottom with the + sign is used to add certificates and keys to the M5Stack controllers however, we can also use UIFlows, file manager dialog to upload keys and certificates to M5Stack controllers. The UIFlow manage is found in the Icons on the top of the screen on the right hand side of UIFlow.

Clicking on this icon will display the manager dialog.

Click on "Certificates " and the certificate folder is opened, clicking "Add Certificate" opens the file dialog opened by clicking the "+" icon on the block. In the above image you can see that I cave the Device Certificate, Private key and Public keys uploaded and named as UIFlow expected them.

The Micropython code for this block is as follows:

from IoTcloud.AWS import AWS

aws = AWS(things_name='', host='', port=0, keepalive=0, cert_file_path='', private_key_path='')

This is just a set of instructions that define setting that code will need to know in order to work.

AWS Start

The AWS start block is used to start AWS dedicated code. This block must be placed outside and before the main programming loop or AWS will think it is some kind of attack and block the repeated service creation calls.

AWS SubScribe

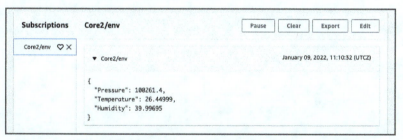

The AWS Subscribe is a standalone function loop that runs independent to our main AWS code once a connection to the AWS IoT service has been established. The Block will attempt to connect to an AWS topic and download data from it.

Subscriptions	Core2/env			Pause	Clear	Export	Edit

```
Subscriptions    Core2/env                        Pause    Clear    Export    Edit

Core2/env  ♥ ✕
                  ▼ Core2/env                          January 09, 2022, 11:10:32 (UTCZ)

                  {
                    "Pressure": 100261.4,
                    "Temperature": 26.44999,
                    "Humidity": 39.99695
                  }
```

The Above screenshot is the topic the AWS IoT test server used by the demo I will share later in this section.

Get Topic Data

Get topic_data

The Get Topic Data block is used within the AWS Subscribe function loop to allow an M5Stack controller to read data sent to the AWS IoT server.

In this example I am using a label to display data from the AWS IoT topic on the M5Stack screen. In the following photo you can see how the data is displayed on the screen of an M5Stack.

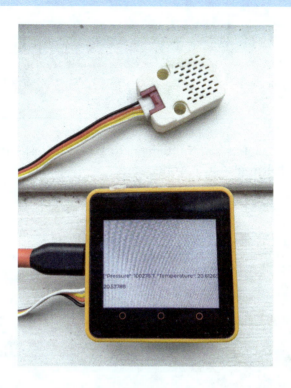

Publish Topic

The Publish Topic block is used to send data to an AWS service. The first space is for a text block containing the topic and the second space is for the data. Data can be plain text but its better if it is JSON formatted data for example:

This is another snippet from the example that just shows how the Publish Topic block works.

This is the complete program for reading data from the M5Stack ENVIII Unit and sending it to AWS IoT.

The Micropython code for this is shown on the next page.

```
from m5stack import *
from m5stack_ui import *
from uiflow import *
from IoTcloud.AWS import AWS
import json

import time
import unit

screen = M5Screen()
```

```
screen.clean_screen()
screen.set_screen_bg_color(0xFFFFFF)
env3_0 = unit.get(unit.ENV3, unit.PORTA)

label0 = M5Label('Text', x=-2, y=147, color=0x000,
font=FONT_MONT_14, parent=None)
label1 = M5Label('Text', x=0, y=176, color=0x000,
font=FONT_MONT_14, parent=None)

def fun_Core2_env_(topic_data):
  # global params
  label0.set_text(str(topic_data))
  pass


aws = AWS(things_name='CORE2', host='a7lxppddpjt7e-
ats.iot.eu-west-2.amazonaws.com', port=8883, keepalive=60,
cert_file_path="/flash/res/certificate.pem.crt",
private_key_path="/flash/res/private.pem.key")

aws.subscribe(str('Core2/env'), fun_Core2_env_)
aws.start()
while True:
  aws.publish(str('Core2/env'),str((json.dumps(({'Temperature':
(env3_0.temperature),'Humidity':(env3_0.humidity),'Pressure':
(env3_0.pressure)})))))
  label1.set_text(str(env3_0.temperature))
  wait(4)
  wait_ms(2)
```

MQTT

Introduction.

So far I have shown you how to use IoT services that have dedicated blocks available in UIFlow. In this section I will show you how to connect to other services using the MQTT blocks available in UIFlow.

As always, we start with the basic program:

Next we add the MQTT "Set Client ID" block.

MQTT Credentials

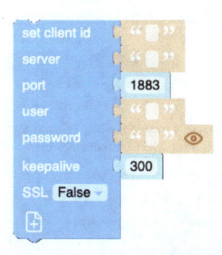

The MQTT Credentials block is used to hold the access credentials needed to log into an MQTT server as well as assign any SSL certificates that may be required to access the MQTT servers. These credentials are as follows:

Set Client ID need to be a unique name for each device otherwise, if you try to reuse the Client stream the stream will be immediately disconnected preventing both devices from access the stream.

Server is the MQTT/IoT server address.

Port is set to 1883 by default,

User is the user name you used to registered with an MQTT/IoT service.

Password hold the Server access password or access key.

Keep Alive is used to maintain a connection to a MQTT service. Some services will automatically close the connection between an IoT device and service if no data is received after a short time.

SSL is used if the IOT service provides SSL encryption certificates and keys. Setting this to true brings up additional boxes that allow you to assign the various certificates.

MQTT Start

Next we have the MQTT Start block:

This block is used to start the MQTT service on the Core2 and goes directly after the MQTT Credentials block:

Publish to Topic with Message

In order to send data to an MQTT Server we need to use:

The Topic is where the data is to be listed and the message contains the data/telemetry from the sensor connected to the Core2.

In the following sample of code based on the previous example: the temperature reading from the ENV3 unit are send to the Temperature topic:

```
[+]
mqtt start
Set Watering_0 ▾ pump status ▶ 0
Loop
    publish topic  " Temperature "  msg  Get env3_0 ▾ Temperature
    Label label0 ▾ show    Get env3_0 ▾ Pressure
    Label label1 ▾ show    Get env3_0 ▾ Temperature
    Label label2 ▾ show    Get env3_0 ▾ Humidity
```

The sample shows that I have just added the publish block to the beginning of the loop before the label blocks.

MQTT Subscribe with Topic Data

In order to receive data/telemetry from the MQTT server, we first need to subscribe to a topic using the following block:

The MQTT Subscribe block is a loop function that constantly checks a specified subject for updated data/telemetry.

Get Topic Data

In order to display the data/telemetry retrieved we use the Get Topic Data block:

The Get Topic block only returns the data as a value and so need to be placed in a block like a label block in order to display the data on the Core2's Screen.

The following example when added to the current program and run will show the retrieved temperature reading at the bottom of the Core2's screen.

Set Last Will Topic Message

Adafruit IO

Introduction.

Adafruit IO is an IoT/MQTT service provided by Adafruit industries and has been designed to allow quick and easy setup and connection of hardware to the internet.

Unlike AWS and Azure (as of this book going to press) adafruit.io does not have dedicated UIFlow blocks. Over the next sever pages I will show you how to use UIFlows MQTT blocks to connect to the adafruit.io servers.

To. Use the Adafruit IO servers you need to register for a free account or if yo u are already registered on Adafruit.com website you just sign in.

Once you register or sign in you will be taken to the profile page:

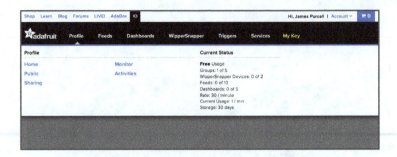

In order to send data to io.adafruit.com you need to create a feed. Click on Feed and you will be taken to the Feed page:

Next click on "View All" to be taken to the feed editor:

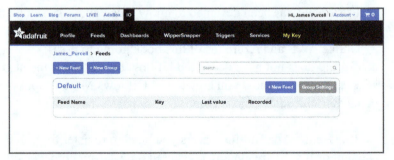

This page shows that there are no feeds and so we need to click on "New Feed" to create one:

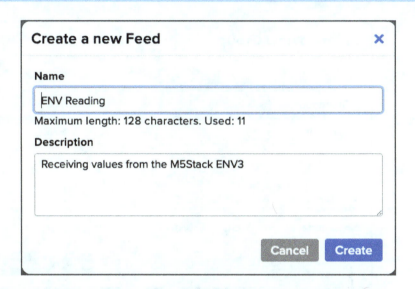

Enter a name for the feed and give the feed a description. Click on "Create" and you will be returned to the feed screen with the new feed listed:

We can also create groups of feeds by clicking on the 'Create Group" button and naming it like we did for the feed:

Click on create and a feed group will appear under feeds:

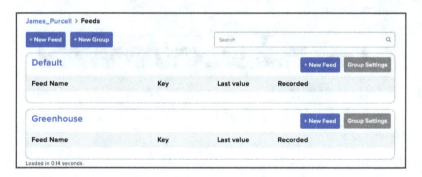

Now click on the "+ New Feed" button in the group box and add separate feeds for the data streams we will be sending:

Now that we have created the feeds, we need to create a dashboard to show the feed. To do that, click on "Dashboard" to open the Dashboard Page:

Like with the flow page, this shows that there is no dashboard set up and so we need to click on "View All" in order to get the dashboard editor:

Click on the "New Dashboard" button to open the dashboard dialog and give it a name and description:

Click on the "Create" button and adafruit.io will return to the dashboard screen showing our newly created dashboard:

Click on the newly created "Environmental Dashboard" and the dashboard editor will open:

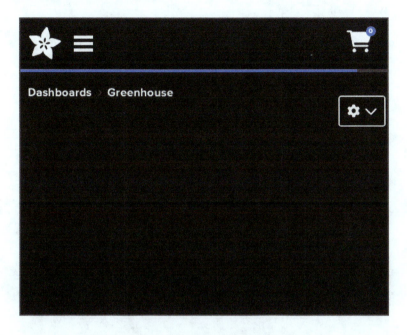

Click on the gear shape to open the dashboard menu:

Now click on the "Create New Block" and the block window will open:

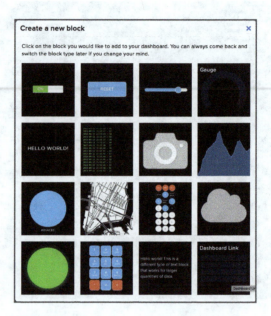

Click on the "Stream" block and the next window will ask you to chose a feed:

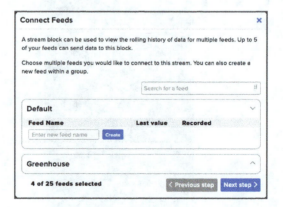

As you can see in the previous image, there are no feeds visible but there is the Greenhouse group. Click on the arrow to the right of Greenhouse to open the grouped feeds:

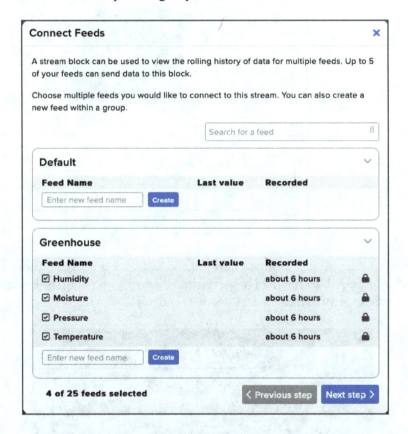

Click on the box's next to the feeds to select them and the button on the bottom will now change to "Next Step" Click on it and the settings window will appear:

Leave all the setting as they are and just click on "Create Block" and we will be returned to the dashboard screen showing the blank block ready to receive data that we send to it.

That is everything we need to set up on the io.adafruit.com side of things and so now we can move on to the M5Stack UIFlow code side.

To send data to io.adafruit.com we will use the MQTT blocks found in UIFLOW.

Starting with the Sample code from the MQTT section:

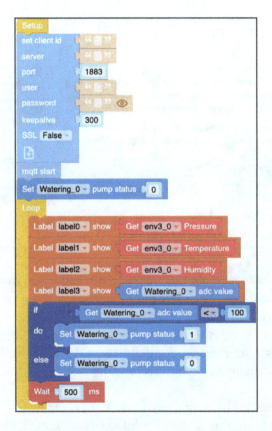

Enter the details into the configuration block as follows.

Set Client ID need to be a unique name for each device otherwise, if you try to reuse the Client stream the stream will be immediately disconnected preventing both devices from access the stream.

Server is io.adafruit.com.

Port is set to 1883 by default for none secure connections and 8883 for SSL encrypted connections.

User is the user name you used to registered <u>adafruit.io</u>

Password in Adafruit's case is the key you download from the key window

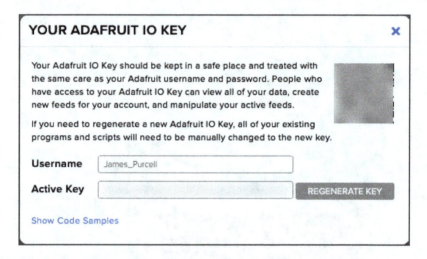

Keep Alive is used to maintain a connection to a MQTT service. Some services will automatically close the connection between an IOT device and service if no data is received after a short time.

SSL is used if the IoT service provides SSL encryption certificates and keys. Unfortunately <u>io.adafruit.com</u> doesn't provide these (or I'm yet to find them) and so this is set to false.

When asked about certificate and key files Adafruit can be a little reserved when answering and will point too examples that use a secure connection without these files.

Next we add the Publish Topic block before the Label blocks and set the topic to the MQTT Feed address found By clicking on the gear next to Feed Info that will bring up the following:

Copy the link (highlighted) next to MQTT by Key and paste it into the topic space and replace for all four of the sensors data streams.

For the sake of simplicity, I have removed the pump control blocks in order to concentrate on only the data being sent to Adafruit.io.

If we click on each of the feeds we can see a chart of the data streams but when we go back to the dashboard we get a data throttle warning. This is an issue with the free service of adafruit.io and is cause by four data streams being sent at the same time.
Unfortunately the only way around this is to remove three of the streams leaving on the temperature stream available.

Now if we go into adafruit.io and view the dashboard we see live the live data appearing without a throttle warning.

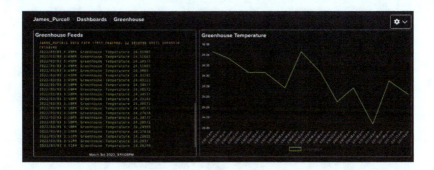

Here I have added a line graph to show how the temperature is fluctuating.

Useful Forms.

Azure IoT Planner

Display Name	Name	Capability	Semantic Type	Schema
Shown as Data type Heading.	Data Type Name.	Property, Telemetry, Command	Type of reading (Temp, Pressure,Speed, etc)	Double, Float, Integra or Long
Temperature	Temperature	Telemetry	Temperature	Double
Water Pump	Pump	Command	N/A	N/A

You are free to Copy and print this form for private use.

Access Key List.

Azure Primary Access Key: ....

Azure Secondary Access Key: ....

Azure Stream End Points:..

....

....

....

....

....

....

....

EZData Access Token: ....

....

....

MQTT User ID: ....

MQTT Pasword: ....

....

MQTT Access Key if required (replaces password): ....

....

....

....

MQTT Notes: ....

....

....

....

....

....

....

....

....

....

....

....

In Closing.

Thank you for taking the time to read through my guide. If you have any questions, please feel free to ask and I will put the answer in the next update of the book that is due after the UIFlow 2.X update.

If you have any ideas and suggestions on improving these guides please let me know.

If you found this guide useful you can subscribe to my Youtube channel found here:
https://www.youtube.com/channel/UCn5qzjLQdVz9K8SM0ojJAEA

You can find me on hackster.io here: https://www.hackster.io/AJB2K3

In the official FB group here: https://www.facebook.com/groups/m5stack

On the Official forums found here: https://community.m5stack.com